Origins

Ducks

Alex Lane
Character illustrations by Jonatronix

OXFORD
UNIVERSITY PRESS

Ducks

dad

mum

baby ducks

The duck has a nest.

The duck sits on the nest.

The duck has eggs.

The duck sits on the eggs.

Later ...

Look!

The eggs hatch.

The baby ducks are born.

The baby ducks grow.

Look at him swim.

The baby ducks can swim.

Find out more

Read about more families in ...